WOMEN
AND WAR

WOMEN AND WAR

ANN KRAMER

SEA-TO-SEA
Mankato Collingwood London

Designer Jason Billin
Editor Sarah Ridley
Art Director Jonathan Hair
Editor-in-Chief John C. Miles
Picture research Diana Morris

Picture credits
Bettmann/Corbis: 25
Cody Images: cover, 2, 8, 11, 16, 19, 20, 30, 31
John Hinde Archive/HIP/Topham: 9
Peter Newark's Pictures:
  10, 12 detail © DACS London 2005, 18
Picturepoint/Topham: 7, 15, 23, 28, 32
Picture Post/GettyImages: 27
PRO/HIP Topham: 14

*Every attempt has been made to clear copyright.
Should there be any inadvertent omission please
apply to the publisher for rectification.*

Note to parents and teachers:
Every effort has been made by the Publishers to
ensure that the web sites in this book are suitable
for children, that they are of the highest
educational value, and that they contain no
inappropriate or offensive material. However,
because of the nature of the Internet, it is
impossible to guarantee that the contents of these
sites will not be altered. We strongly advise that
Internet access be supervised by a responsible
adult.

This edition first published in 2009 by
Sea-to-Sea Publications
Distributed by Black Rabbit Books
P.O. Box 3263
Mankato, Minnesota 56002

Copyright © Sea-to-Sea Publications 2009

Printed in China

Library of Congress Cataloging-in-Publication Data:

Kramer, Ann.
  Women and war / Ann Kramer.
    p. cm. -- (World War Two)
  Includes index.
  Summary: "Discusses the role of women from the Allied countries during World
War II, including those who served in the armed forces, those who took over men's
jobs at home, and more"--Provided by publisher.
  ISBN 978-1-59771-142-5
  1. World War, 1939-1945--Participation, Female--Juvenile literature. 2. World
War, 1939-1945--Women--Juvenile literature. 3. Women and war. I. Title.
  D810.W7K69 2009
  940.53'32082--dc22
                                        2008007832

9 8 7 6 5 4 3 2

Published by arrangement with the Watts Publishing
Group Ltd, London.

CONTENTS

Setting the Scene

World War II (1939–45) was a total war. It involved not just troops but also civilians. Women played an essential part. For some, life would never be the same again.

Peace and Poppies

Some women and women's organizations campaigned for peace between the wars. They included British feminist Dora Russell (1894–1986), the Women's International League for Peace and Freedom (WILPF), and the Women's Freedom League. In 1933 the Women's Co-operative Guild together with the Peace Pledge Union (PPU) created a white poppy. Like the red poppy, it was worn on November 11 to honor the dead of World War One but it also stood for peace. Some people still wear it today.

> **❝ I held my chin high and kept back the tears at the thought of the slaughter ahead.❞**
>
> *Female schoolteacher, on hearing British Prime Minister Chamberlain announce the declaration of war on the radio.*

Experience of War

Women had been involved in war before; thousands of women rallied to the war effort during World War I (1914–18). In that first global conflict, women took over when men left home to fight. They worked in factories making weapons, drove buses, and harvested the land, doing so-called "men's work" for the very first time. They nursed the wounded on the front line. In every way, women challenged the image of what women were supposed to be. Most women also lost men close to them—fathers, brothers, husbands, sons, and friends who died in the trenches.

Changing Lives

After 1918, women were expected to give up work and return to the home. Most did. But nothing was quite the same again. Women's lives began to change, particularly in Britain and America. They had proved themselves as citizens and now gained the vote—something they had been demanding since the 1840s. By 1931, there were seven women Representatives and one Senator in the U.S. Congress.

Around the world millions of women were in paid employment. Most were in low-paid jobs but there were greater opportunities. Women could be civil servants, work in law, and serve on juries. Even so, there was a clear division between what people thought was "men's work" and "women's work." Women were definitely expected to give up work when they married.

Women in the late 1930s had more rights than in 1914 but they were not equal with men. People still thought a woman's place was in the home and that a husband should support his wife.

Preparing for War

Europe had been preparing for war since 1938. Many people hoped it would not happen. The horrors and losses of World War I were too close. Some women had campaigned for peace between the wars. However, as war became inevitable women knew they would have to play their part. In fact, far more women would be involved in World War II than in World War I.

A family tries out its gas masks. During World War II, everybody in Britain had to carry a mask in case the Germans dropped bombs containing poison gas.

Votes for Women

Between 1918–39 Women in many countries gained the vote

1918 British women over the age of 30 gain the vote; women over 21 can be Members of Parliament (MPs)

1918 Austrian, Hungarian, Latvian, and Lithuanian women gain the vote

1919 German and Polish women gain the vote

1920 American, Czechoslovakian, and Albanian women gain the vote

1928 British women over 21 have the right to vote on an equal basis with men

1932 Spanish and Thai women have the vote

1934 Brazilian and Cuban women have the vote

Volunteering to Help

On September 3, 1939, Britain and its empire declared war on Germany after German troops invaded Poland. World War II had begun. In Britain thousands of women offered their help.

Women ambulance-service volunteers practice carrying stretchers in 1939. Their skills would soon be needed after the Luftwaffe (German air force) began to bomb British cities.

Women in Nazi Germany

German women had the vote but the National Socialist (Nazi) Party did not believe in women's rights. Women joined the Party and there was a Nazi Women's League. Girls and young women joined the Hitler Youth and the German Girls' League. They were told their main job was to be good wives and produce children. Women with large families were awarded a Cross of Motherhood.

Volunteers in every Field

British women volunteered to be nurses, ambulance drivers, and air-raid wardens. Some joined the Auxiliary Territorial Army (ATS), which was formed in 1938. Many women, particularly older women or those with small children, could not do full-time work. Instead, they joined voluntary organizations.

Women's Voluntary Service (WVS)

The largest women's voluntary organization was the Women's Voluntary Service (WVS). It was formed in 1938, with just five members. By 1941 the WVS had more than one million members throughout Britain, most of them middle-class women.

The WVS gave help wherever it was needed on the "Home Front." In September 1939, WVS women in distinctive gray-green uniforms helped evacuate children out of the cities, away from the risk of air raids. It was a huge job. More than one million children were evacuated in just three days.

Food, Clothing, and Comfort

When air raids pulverized British cities the WVS worked with civil defense workers to care for bombed-out civilians. They set up mobile canteens, organized rest centers, and found temporary housing for people whose homes had been destroyed. They distributed clothing parcels—Bundles for Britain—from Canada and the United States. The WVS also provided tea, snacks, and cigarettes for thousands of soldiers. When they were not on call, the WVS, like women in all the warring countries, knitted countless balaclava helmets, scarves, gloves, and socks for servicemen. Membership in the American Women's Voluntary Service (AWVS) grew as women volunteered for wartime relief work, helping the families of servicemen fighting abroad.

"*...Nobody is more welcome to the 'bombed-out,' wardens and demolition workers than the WVS with their mobile canteens. Now there is a bite to eat and a cup of tea to hearten them. That's only one of the jobs WVS do, voluntarily... and they nearly all have homes to run as well.***"**

Text from 1944 advertisement aiming to recruit British women for the WVS.

An American Women's Voluntary Service (AWVS) relief worker helps a girl choose a dress from a clothing bank in 1944.

Calling all Women

From 1939 to 1945 millions of women entered the labor force. As men went off to fight, women replaced them as workers. Their contribution to the war effort was huge.

THE SATURDAY EVENING POST

MAY 29, 1943   10¢

BEGINNING—A NEW KELLAND SERIAL
Heart on Her Sleeve

EDGAR SNOW REPORTS ON GERMAN ATROCITIES

U.S. artist Norman Rockwell's 1943 picture of factory worker "Rosie the Riveter" became one of the most famous images of World War II.

Opening doors

War work created new opportunities for women. In Britain and the United States married women entered the work force in huge numbers, something that would have been unthinkable before the war. In the USA at least 400,000 black women worked in manufacturing for the first time. Before that they could only work as domestic servants or on the land.

A Slow Start

When war began, men were immediately called up for armed service. Women were needed—to produce food, weapons, warships, uniforms, and the other necessities of war. British women volunteered but the government was slow to use them. Many women were told to stay at home or in the jobs they had unless they were particularly qualified. The Women's Freedom League complained bitterly that "the Government is not making anything like the full use of the Woman Power of the country."

Conscripting Women

By 1941 Britain desperately needed at least a million more workers. Government propaganda and radio broadcasts urged women to come into the factories and "do their bit." From December the government formally conscripted (drafted) women. Britain was the first country ever to do this.

First, only single women aged 20–30 were called up. Later, all women aged 19–51 were conscripted. By 1943, nine out of ten single women and eight out of ten married women were in the forces, Land Army, or war industries. The total number of British women in war work was about 7,750,000—two million more than in 1939.

Around the World

The Soviet Union drafted millions of women into essential war work. Mobilization of women was greater there than anywhere as women replaced the 20 million men who left to fight. In the United States, posters featuring Rosie the Riveter or Wanda the Welder helped to bring more than six million women into the work force. In Australia, New Zealand, Canada, and South Africa women were also recruited for wartime production. In Germany, however, women were not recruited until late in the war.

Types of Work

Women did every job imaginable— on railroads, on the land, in transportation, and in factories. They worked as engineers, builders, welders, electricians, and chemists. Many were doing jobs once thought only suitable for men.

Canadian First

Some Canadian women worked on assembly lines producing military aircraft. Elsie MacGill (1905–80) supervised one of the assembly plants. She was the first Canadian woman to graduate as an electrical engineer and the world's first female aeronautical designer. Her staff produced about 1,450 Hawker Hurricane fighter aircraft. Some were used in the Battle of Britain (Aug–Oct 1940).

Thousands of women worked in munitions factories during the war. These women workers are making huge bombs to be dropped from aircraft.

Hard-working Women

Recruitment posters showed factory work as glamorous and desirable. The reality was different. Women worked long hours in difficult conditions. Many looked after a home, too.

This picture, Ruby Loftus screwing a Breech-ring, *was painted by Dame Laura Knight in 1943. It shows gun factory worker Ruby Loftus performing a task that required great precision. Male colleagues were amazed that a woman could do this better than they.*

For and Against

Wartime production of weapons, tanks, aircraft, warships, submarines, parachutes, and uniforms would not have been possible without women. However, not everyone wanted women to work. Prime Minister Winston Churchill thought it would damage family life. One man said: "home life would vanish" and "men will come back to cold and untidy homes, with no meal ready." Male labor unionists and workers saw women as a threat to their wages and a man's role as head of the family. Most women, however, wanted to work.

> **"** *She's the girl*
> *That makes the thing*
> *That drills the hole*
> *That holds the spring*
> *That drives the rod*
> *That turns the knob*
> *That works the*
> *thingumabob...*
> *That's going to win*
> *the war* **"**
>
> *World War II popular song*

Working Conditions

Women without families—usually young, single women—could be sent anywhere they were needed. They lived in hostels. Those with families worked nearer to home.

Factory women worked 60 or more hours a week with only short breaks for lunch and tea. Some had only one weekend off in three. Women complained that factory work was boring and repetitive. The noise of machines was deafening and women worked in dirty, dangerous conditions, sometimes without ventilation or light because of the blackout. There were often no washrooms for women. Women who had worked before the war knew what to expect but new workers were often shocked. Munitions workers had to use explosive and toxic materials. Some lost fingers or hands if there was an accident. Air raids added to the danger. Women often had to keep working until the last minute before diving for shelter.

A Double Burden

After a long day's work, women with families had to go home to cook and clean. They needed to shop, which meant lining up. As war progressed, some employers set up nurseries and childcare centers, and introduced flexible working hours. Women's washrooms were also installed.

Skills and Pay

During the war women earned more than ever before, particularly in skilled work on the railroads, in shipbuilding, aircraft production, and engineering. Even so, they earned less than men, sometimes as low as half a man's wage for the same work. There were complaints and in 1943, skilled women workers who were earning less than male cleaners went on strike in Glasgow, Scotland. But actions like this were rare.

Dressing the part

War work had a big impact on women's clothes. A factory was no place for fashion. Women donned smocks and suspenders, overalls and trousers to keep clean. For safety, they covered their hair in bandanas or scarves made into turbans, something that became a key wartime image.

"*A bomb hit the factory before we were given permission to go to the shelter. The paint department went up. I saw several people flying through the air and I just ran home. I was suffering from shock.*"

Muriel Simkin, munitions worker

On the Land

In Britain, many women worked on the land. It was hard, backbreaking work. Most had never done farm work before but their efforts kept food supplies flowing.

Women's Land Army

In 1939 the Women's Land Army (WLA) was formed. It had existed in World War I but was disbanded in 1919. Now, as men left farms to fight, it was needed again. By 1944, some 90,000 women had joined. Most were young. They were known as Land Girls. Women in Australia, Canada, the United States, and the USSR also did essential work on the land.

'We could do with thousands more like you..'

JOIN THE
WOMEN'S LAND ARMY

Apply to NEAREST W·L·A COUNTY OFFICE or to W·L·A HEADQUARTERS 6, CHESHAM STREET, LONDON S.W.1

A recruiting poster urges British women to help farmers by joining the Women's Land Army.

Real-life recruitment

Recruitment posters usually showed romanticized pictures of land workers. They never looked quite real. One poster did feature a real Land Girl. Her name was Mary Feddon. During her training someone photographed her with a newborn calf. She could not find the negative. To her surprise, she later saw her picture on a Land Army recruitment poster.

Work, Pay, and Conditions

Many young women came from cities and towns. They had been office or shop workers, hairdressers, or in other jobs that had nothing to do with farming. Some were conscientious objectors. They were given a medical checkup, perhaps some training, then sent to work in the countryside. They lived in hostels or on farms. Some stayed in old workers' cottages without running water, gas, or electricity.

Land Girls worked 50-hour weeks for very little pay. They drove tractors, planted and harvested, spread manure, and dug ditches. They looked after cattle and poultry and did the milking. They even caught rats to prevent them from destroying crops.

Girls worked from early morning to nightfall. They had Sundays off and a home visit once every six months. Many complained about the food.

At first male farmers thought women would not manage heavy work on the land. They were wrong. By 1943 Land Girls were helping to produce 70 percent of Britain's food.

Lumberjills

About 6,000 women joined the Timber Corps. They were nicknamed "Lumberjills." They did heavy forestry work, felling trees, cutting poles for mineshafts, loading charcoal, and making wooden roads. Land Girls and Lumberjills sometimes worked with Italian prisoners of war (POWs), who were put to work on the land.

In most of the warring countries, women helped with a range of farming work.

" *We were quite a happy crowd.... The food was the worst thing... the way it was cooked... The rice was so hard it was like chicken feed, the potatoes were cooked with the dirt still on them...we only had three sandwiches to last a full day in the woods.* **"**

Annice Gibbs, Timber Corps

Women in the Forces

Women were not allowed to fight but they joined women's sections in all the armed forces: army, navy, and air force.

Charity Adams-Earley

Charity Adams-Earley was the first black American woman to serve as a commissioned officer in the Women's Army Corps. Segregation (separation) of blacks and whites still existed in the United States and few black American women were allowed to join the U.S. forces. Despite prejudice, she became a major and commanded the first unit of black WACs to serve in France.

Knickers or jumpers

Women in the WRNS were known as Wrens. They wore blue serge uniforms. Their knickers (panties) were navy blue too. Some Wrens found a good use for them. "We used to turn the knickers upside down, sew across for shoulder seams, take out the gusset and make them into jumpers (sweaters)."

Women's Services

British women joined the Auxiliary Territorial Service (ATS), the women's section of the army, the Women's Royal Naval Service (WRNS) or the Women's Auxiliary Air Force (WAAF). There was also the Women's Transport Service. By 1943 more than 500,000 women were serving in the ATS, WRNS, and WAAF combined.

American women served in the Women's Army Corps (WAC), and were sent to all theaters of war. They joined the women's section of the navy, which was known as WAVES—Women Accepted for Voluntary Service—as well as the marines and coastguards. Canadian and Australian women also served in their armed forces. The shortage of manpower in Germany meant that German women, too, were enlisted into the forces.

Lined up for inspection: women of the WAAF on parade in 1943.

Noncombat Duties

Women were not allowed to fight but they wore uniforms and learned to drill and take orders just like men. They worked as drivers, cooks, and clerks, freeing men to fight. As war progressed, they did more. In Britain the WAAFs and WRNS worked in command centers and operation rooms as telephone operators or using radar and wireless to plot the movement of ships and planes. Sometimes operation rooms were bombed but the women kept on working. Occasionally, they had the horrible experience of hearing pilots screaming as their planes went down in flames.

Antiaircraft Guns

Women worked alongside men on antiaircraft guns, known in Britain as ack-ack. It was heavy, dangerous work. Women moved the searchlights to light up incoming planes so they could be shot down, which made them targets as well. They positioned the guns but were not allowed to fire them. The WRNS were not allowed on fighting ships but operated heavy launches and overhauled depth charges and torpedoes.

British women served in France, Egypt, and Asia. In 1940, ATS switchboard operators were among the last to be evacuated from Dunkirk.

Fighting Women

Some women did fight. Russian women fought on the front in artillery and tank units. Some were snipers. Uniformed Polish women fought against invading German troops and an all-woman Indian regiment called the Rani fought in Burma. In Germany, women's fighting battalions were created toward the end of the war.

MILITARY WOMEN

Britain

Some 500,000 enlisted in the services during the war. In 1943, more than 56,000 were in antiaircraft command.
Women in the services in 1943 were:
- WRNS 180,000
- WAAF 180,000
- ATS 210,000

Canada

More than 45,000 volunteered for military service.

Australia

About 78,000 joined war services.

United States

Nearly 400,000 women served in the U.S. military, including 800 Native Americans.
Summer 1943 figures were:
- WACs 100,000
- WAVES 92,000
- Marines 20,000
- Coastguards (SPARS) 11,000
- WASPs (Women's air force) 1,000
- Army Nurse Corps 57,000
- Navy Nurse Corps 11,000

Soviet Union

About 800,000 served in the Red Army. 300,000 belonged to antiaircraft units.

Germany

450,000 joined auxiliary services. 65,000—100,000 served in antiaircraft units.

Airborne Women

Most women who joined the air force worked on the ground at airfields or in communications centers. Some women flew and ferried planes. Soviet women fought in the skies.

Flying Heroine

In 1940 the *Girl's Own Paper*, a British comic for girls, featured an exciting new heroine—Worrals of the WAAF. Her adventures appeared throughout the war. Unlike a real WAAF member, Worrals flew fighter planes as well as transport. She even shot down an enemy aircraft. Worrals possibly helped recruit a lot of young women into the WAAF.

Pilots of the WAAF.

Joining the Air Force

By 1943 some 180,000 British women had joined the Women's Auxiliary Air Force (WAAF). Thousands of Canadian women joined the Women's Division of the Royal Canadian Air Force when it was formed in 1941. In 1943 more than 1,000 women joined the elite Women's Air Service Pilots (WASPs). German women joined the Luftwaffe.

Women were not allowed to fly combat missions. Most worked on the ground, providing support for male fighter pilots. Some worked as electricians and mechanics. Others worked in aerial photography units and as "plotters," working in new radar stations tracking incoming bombers. Women packed parachutes and developed navigation skills. WAAFs staffed barrage balloons.

Flying Role

There were skilled women pilots. They could not take part in combat but they flew planes from factories to airfields and squadrons wherever they were needed. In Britain, the Air Transport Auxiliary (ATA) was formed in 1939 to do this work. Nearly half the ATA pilots were women. They included famous British pilot Amy Johnson. Canadian and American women also flew with the ATA including the American aviator, Jackie Cochran, who later formed the WASPs.

Women flew all sorts of planes, including Spitfires, Hurricanes, and large bombers. They were not always welcome. The male editor of the flying magazine *Aeroplane* said women pilots were a "menace." In fact ATA women had far fewer crashes than men.

In the United States more than 900 WASPs ferried more than 12,000 aircraft from factories to airfields. They towed gliders and targets and flew practice missions to train bomber crews. Like their British counterparts, WASPs were discriminated against. They remained civilians and their role was not formally recognized until 1977.

Night Witches

The Soviet Union was the first country to allow women to fly combat missions. In 1941, Russian pilot Marina Raskova created three all-women air combat squadrons: a fighter squadron, a short-range dive-bomber squadron, and a night fighter-bomber squadron. The night fighters became known as the "Night Witches." In ramshackle biplanes, the Night Witches flew 24,000 night bombing raids over German front lines, targeting railroads, ammunition dumps, and artillery positions.

Decorated for Bravery

In May 1940 Joan Daphne Mary Pearson became the first WAAF to be decorated for outstanding bravery. She was awarded the George Cross for pulling an RAF pilot from a burning plane and using her body to shield him from a 120-pound (55kg) bomb that exploded nearby. She survived and saved his life.

A woman pilot prepares to take off and deliver a much-needed aircraft to a front-line squadron.

Nurses

Women had nursed the wounded in World War I. Now nurses were needed for World War II. Many served on the front lines.

Military and Civilian

Thousands of women in the warring nations came forward as nurses. Some were part of the military, attached mainly to the army but also with the air force and navy. They were subject to military rules and discipline.

There were also civilian nurses—professional or volunteers. British women worked with the Red Cross, the Voluntary Aid Detachment (VAD), or other nonmilitary groups.

Nurses on all the warring sides often worked in appalling and dangerous conditions.

> ❝ *There were stretchers all down the middle of the tent, there were charred bodies everywhere, some were quiet and dying, others screaming with pain, all with severe burns.* ❞
>
> Iris Ogilvia, Canadian nurse

On the Front Line

Nurses worked at home and abroad. In Britain, nurses on the home front worked in general hospitals, special units treating facial or other injuries, and first-aid centers. They treated air-raid victims and wounded soldiers back from the front.

In World War I, nurses were not supposed to work near the front line, though many did. In World War II, it was policy to send nurses as close to the front line as possible. As a result, they were exposed to more dangers than almost any other women in the war. During Dunkirk, 1,300 British nurses dressed the wounded in the open while the beaches were bombed.

Nurses went to war zones in Europe, North Africa, and the Far East. Some worked in field or evacuation hospitals. These were traveling units where nurses gave emergency treatment to the wounded straight off the battlefield. They became skilled at packing up and moving supplies and patients if enemy troops broke through. Nurses also worked in hospitals situated further back from the front line. These were often bombed or abandoned hospitals or schools. They nursed soldiers on hospital trains and ships, and on planes.

Harsh Conditions

Nurses learned to survive and cope in harsh, extremely dangerous and distressing conditions. They worked long hours treating terrible wounds and diseases such as typhus, malaria, and diptheria. They improvised when supplies ran low, reusing bandages or turning trousers into stretchers. Some nurses gave their own blood for transfusions. Hospitals and hospital ships were bombed and nurses were killed. Many allied nurses were taken prisoner by the Japanese and suffered dreadful mistreatment. Some nurses treated survivors of the concentration camps. They were shocked to learn that German nurses had assisted in the Holocaust.

A Nurse's Story

Olwen "Bobbie" Roberts of Southport, Lancashire, joined the Red Cross and was called up in 1940. She was put onto a surgical ward nursing soldiers arriving from Dunkirk. These were "incredibly bad, extensive burns, a lot of amputations." Later, she was sent to York Military Hospital. Air raids were vicious but nurses had to work through. However, there were amusing moments. "During an air raid, we were expected to put spare mattresses over the men who were bedridden and fill the baths with water.... I was on my own... I couldn't do it, I was laughing so much and so were the men."

Olwen later joined the VAD. In 1944 she was sent to India to nurse. She traveled by sea in a huge convoy as one of 200 VADs. She was sent to a military hospital in Chittagong, Bengal, where she nursed seriously wounded British and Indian soldiers and gained a reputation for being able to sniff out gangrene. She lived in a bamboo hut called a basha. The work was hard but on time off, "you went to one party or another." In 1946 she returned to England. Of her wartime nursing she says: "I am immensely pleased to have taken part. It was a very important part of my life."

Making Do

Food and clothing were rationed during the war. As war continued, the shortages got worse. Women had to find inventive ways of making do.

Wartime Needs

Women in Britain, France, and Germany were most affected by shortages. Even so, women in the USA, New Zealand, Australia, and Canada were also urged to make do and mend because their countries' resources were needed for war.

The Kitchen Front

When it came to food, government propaganda was aimed directly at women. The Ministry of Food coined the phrase "kitchen front" to describe women's efforts in the kitchen. The BBC broadcast "kitchen-front advice." To women who were juggling work, home, children, and limited rations, each day must have felt like a battle in itself.

Rationing

Britain introduced food rationing in January 1940. Butter, bacon, and ham were the first to be rationed. By 1942, sugar, tea, jam, milk, cheese, eggs, and cooking oil were also rationed. As German submarines sank more and more Allied ships, imported fruit such as bananas disappeared completely.

As persons often solely responsible for running the home, women had to produce wholesome, nourishing meals with dried eggs and milk, home-grown fruit and vegetables, and limited amounts of meat and fish. A Ministry of Food was set up and bombarded women with advice on how to cook with wartime rations. Radio programs, pamphlets, and cookbooks advised women to use carrots or apples for sweeteners and recommended dishes like bread pudding or lentil sausages—sausage-shaped items that had no meat in them at all. Restrictions pushed British women's resources to the limit but, in fact, the wartime diet was highly nutritious.

Waste not, Want not

From 1941 clothes were rationed or at least put on a points system. Each person had a certain number of points; different clothes had different point values. Instead of buying new clothes, women mended and reused. They unpicked old woolen clothes and reused the wool to make socks, balaclavas helmets, and anything else they could think of. Knitting became a national pastime as women knitted in air-raid shelters, at work, and anywhere they could find time.

Women made skirts from men's pants, created a sweater by adding knitted sleeves to a vest, or made a blouse from dusters. Nothing was thrown away or wasted. The WVS set up clothes exchanges while government propaganda urged women to "make do and mend." In Germany, where women experienced severe shortages from 1941, women darned clothes with dyed string when thread ran out.

Beets and Tea

Makeup became scarce. Instead of lipstick, women used beet juice to stain their lips. There were no stockings, so women went bare legged or stained their legs with cold tea or gravy browning. Stockings had seams up the back of the leg, so women drew seams onto the back of their legs with an eyebrow pencil.

Making jam

The Women's Institute (WI), a long-established women's voluntary organization, was famous for making jam and preserves. In 1941 they made more than 2,000 tons of preserves from home-grown fruit. The WI also harvested rosehips, which were made into a vitamin-rich syrup for children.

Standing in line in all kinds of weather to buy food for their families was a common wartime experience for millions of women.

Behind the Scenes

Women worked behind the scenes as code-breakers or with highly secret information. Others were secret agents or resistance fighters.

Noor Inayat Khan

Noor Inayat Khan, a descendant of Tipu Sultan, a Muslim ruler of India, was born in the Soviet Union. Her family settled in France. When Germany invaded France, she escaped to England and worked with the Red Cross, then the WAAF. She became a special agent, nicknamed Madeleine, and was flown to France in 1943.

She joined an underground network as a wireless operator and kept working even when members of the network were caught. Ultimately the Gestapo arrested and interrogated her and sent her to Dachau concentration camp. There she and three other women agents—Yolande Beekmann, Elaine Plewman, and Madeleine Damerment— were murdered by the SS.

Breaking the Code

Women were involved in top-secret work. About 2,000 women worked at Bletchley Park, the British Government's Code and Cipher School. Using what was called the "Enigma" machine, an early computer, they learned to decode messages coming in from Germany. Women switchboard operators and secretaries were among the staff at the Cabinet War Office in London. No one could talk about the work they were doing.

Special Operations

By 1940 Germany had occupied France. The British government set up what was known as Special Operations Executive (SOE) to send secret agents into France to help the French underground resistance. Women were recruited to help. Many came from the First Aid Nursing Yeomanry (FANY), an elite women's organization first created in 1907. At first they were code-breakers and created forged documents that could be used in occupied Europe. Then, starting in 1942 they were sent into occupied territories as secret agents. In all, the SOE sent 470 agents into France, 39 of whom were women.

It was extremely dangerous work. Agents were trained, given false names and identities, and parachuted into occupied territories to make contact with the underground. Many carried wireless transmitters. If captured by the Gestapo, they faced torture and execution.

An estimated 200 agents lost their lives; 15 of them were women. They included Noor Inayat Khan (see box), Odette Sansom, Violette Szabo, and Yvonne Rudelat.

Resistance Fighters

Women throughout occupied Europe joined resistance movements and partisan groups to fight against the Germans. They included Jewish women such as Vitka Kempner and Ruzka Korezak and Frenchwomen such as Elaine Mordeaux, a top French resistance commander, who led a unit of 200 fighters. She and her unit held up a German tank advance during the D-Day offensive.

Yugoslavian and Hungarian women fought in partisan groups, the first all-woman Yugoslav partisan group being formed in 1942. Some German and Italian women also resisted Nazi control. They included Wilma Lauterwasse-Pflugfelder, who worked with the underground resistance.

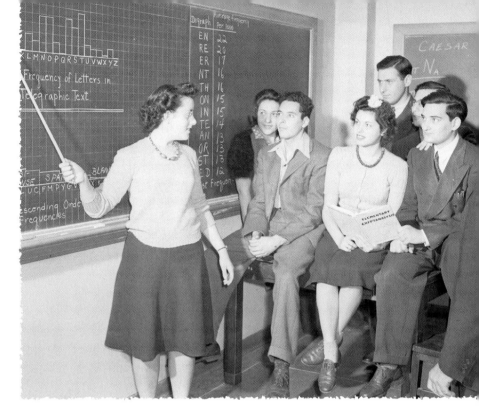

Women played a key role in efforts to break enemy codes. Here, a female lecturer instructs a class at Brooklyn College, New York, on code-breaking techniques, 1942.

> **❝ *I followed the war wherever I could reach it.* ❞**
>
> *Martha Gellhorn, U.S. foreign correspondent who reported from Finland, Hong Kong, Burma, Singapore, and Britain.*

Recording the war

Women journalists, photographers, and artists recorded the war in newspapers, magazines, on radio, and in paintings. Some worked on the front line under fire, before filing their stories to newspapers back home. Sonia Tomara of the *New York Herald Tribune* flew on bombing raids and Margaret Bourke-White of *Life* magazine was torpedoed. Margaret Higgins reported on the concentration camp at Buchenwald. In Britain, Dame Laura Knight worked as an official war artist.

Getting Through

Despite the hardships of war, women managed to enjoy themselves. There were dances, music, humor, and friendships. Professional entertainers boosted morale at home and abroad.

> **"** *We never stopped singing. We knew all the words… We could lose ourselves… forget the horrors of war.* **"**
>
> *Mickie Hulton Storie, ATS*

Lilli Marlene

The most popular song of World War II had a woman's name—Lilli Marlene (Lili Marleen in German). It was based on a love poem written by a German soldier in 1917 and popularized by a Swedish cabaret singer, Lale Andersen. With its haunting words and melody, the song was a favorite with German troops, particularly the Afrika Korps. The British 8th Army heard and adapted the song, which was recorded in English by Anne Shelton. It became equally popular among the Allies.

A Difficult Time

Women's lives were stressful, because war disrupted all aspects of daily life. Work, air raids, food and clothing shortages, keeping a home going, and anxiety about male relatives took their toll. No one knew what the next day would bring. Among the Allies, British women had a long and difficult war.

Despite all this, women still found time to have fun. After the war, many women commented on the close friendships they had made with other women and how people helped each other through difficulties. Jokes—about war, bombs, and wartime food—were part of everyday life.

Music and Dancing

Popular music helped lift morale. Women factory workers in Britain listened to the BBC's *Music While You Work*, which played constantly in factories, even if the noise of machinery sometimes drowned out the sound. In the USA, factories introduced piped music for women workers, who sang along to heart-throb crooners such as Bing Crosby.

After work, women went dancing, sometimes to well known swing or jazz bands. When American soldiers, known as GIs, arrived in Britain, they introduced a new dance craze—the jitterbug. Young women learned eagerly, often dancing with American soldiers, sometimes to the disgust of British men. Thousands of American soldiers took British brides back to the United States after the war.

Women entertainers such as Ivy Benson toured the world doing shows for servicemen.

Entertaining the Troops

Women entertainers boosted morale with live concerts for troops at home and overseas. The British had the Entertainments National Services Association. It was known as ENSA or, for a joke, as Every Night Something Awful. Popular ENSA performers included Gracie Fields, known as "Our Gracie," Anne Shelton, the "force's favorite," and Vera Lynn, the "force's sweetheart." They gave thousands of live performances. Vera Lynn singing "White Cliffs of Dover" became a wartime classic. American entertainers, such as the Andrews Sisters, and superstar Marlene Dietrich toured overseas troop bases and hospitals bringing a taste of home to battle-weary soldiers.

Living for now

Teenagers and young women had more freedom during the war than ever before. They went out on their own or with groups of friends, living life for the moment, and having fun when they could. The future was uncertain and there were many brief love affairs between young women and soldiers.

After the War

The war ended in 1945. Women were exhausted, and many longed for a return to normality. But war had changed women's lives.

Women's Voices

Women's own voices tell us a lot about World War II. Women kept diaries, or wrote letters that give a glimpse of what war was actually like for them at the time. Some women kept diaries for a British study called "Mass Observation." These are stored at Sussex University. Since the war ended, people have recorded women's memories of war as oral history. All these provide valuable insights into women's wartime experiences.

Back into the Home

Some historians believe the Allies would not have won the war without women's contribution. Millions of women had played an essential role. When the war ended, it seemed as if women were no longer needed. Wartime propaganda had urged women to play their part. Now women were told it was their patriotic duty to give up their jobs to men. Images of the "ideal" family showed women in the kitchen, not the factory.

As factories went back to peacetime production, women were laid off or moved back into lower-paid traditional women's jobs. Women welders went back to being typists. One million British women left the workforce. In the United States, three million women came out of work. Some women were pleased to stop.

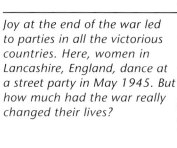

Joy at the end of the war led to parties in all the victorious countries. Here, women in Lancashire, England, dance at a street party in May 1945. But how much had the war really changed their lives?

Others resented giving up their jobs. Widows, whose husbands had been killed, worried about how to support their families.

Independence and Welfare

To start with many women wanted to be housewives again and it looked as if prewar traditions of women being dependent on men would return. In the long run they did not. Divorce rates soared after the war. In 1945 there were twice as many divorces as in 1939. Married women had worked, managed homes, and brought up children single-handedly while their husbands were away. Husbands and wives could not always adjust when peace returned.

Social changes helped women. In 1945 British women received child benefit for the first time, which gave them some financial independence. The Welfare State was introduced, which provided benefits such as free healthcare.

Even after women had been laid off from work in 1945, there were still more women in the labor force than in 1939 and, after a short break, this trend continued. From the 1950s increasing numbers of women, including married women, were entering the labor force.

Equal Rights

During the war women had gained confidence and a sense of their own value. They had proved they were just as capable as men. In the United States, black women had proved they were as able as white women. Women's place in society had changed, even if it was not obvious in 1945. By the 1960s, women worldwide were campaigning for, and demanding, equal rights.

> **"** *During the war we did everything a man could do except fight, and after it was over there was a lot of unrest as well as happiness and sadness, all mixed in together.* **"**
>
> *Canadian woman, RCAF*

Helen Bamber

Helen Bamber was born in London in 1925 to Polish-Jewish parents. In 1945, as the youngest member of UNRRA (United Nations Relief and Rehabilitation Administration), she went into Belsen concentration camp shortly after it was liberated. In 1985 she established the Medical Foundation for the Care of Victims of Torture. Of the war, she says: "I can speak of the fun we had…. I remember laughing and joking during the bombing of London. What I don't like to remember is the fear I had then and the fear I have now that it could all happen again."

Glossary

Allies The United States, Britain, the Soviet Union, and other countries who fought together against Nazi Germany. Germany, Italy, and Japan were known as the Axis powers.

Antiaircraft guns Guns used to shoot down aircraft. Also known as ack-ack.

Auxiliary Someone who provides a supporting role. For example, the Auxiliary Territorial Service (ATS) provided support so that men could go and fight.

Balaclava helmet Covering for the head or neck that leaves only part of the face exposed.

Barrage balloons Huge, hydrogen-filled balloons that floated above cities to protect them from low-flying enemy airplanes. If an aircraft flew too low it would snag in a balloon's cable and crash.

Billeted Being housed in another person's home or in a hostel.

Blackout Switching off all lights at night so that enemy aircraft would not be able to see houses or factories.

British Empire Countries colonized by Britain. By 1939 the Empire still included Canada, Australia, New Zealand, South Africa, and India. They fought with Britain during World War II.

Civilian A woman or man who is an ordinary citizen rather than a member of the armed forces.

Civil defense People, often volunteers, whose work was to defend civilians on the home front.

Conscientious objector A person who, for reasons of conscience, will not fight or join the military.

Conscription Being called up for military service or work.

D-Day June 6, 1944. The day on which Allied forces invaded Nazi-occupied France.

Evacuation Movement of large groups of people from a dangerous place to one of safety.

Gangrene The death and decay of body tissue that sets in when blood flow to the area is interrupted.

Gestapo *Geheimnis Staatspolizei*—the Nazi secret police force.

GI An American soldier. GI stands for Government Issue. American soldiers received GI pants, GI shirts, and various other GI items. In time, they began to call themselves GIs.

Holocaust Term given to the mass murder of Jews by the Nazis during World War II.

Home front A term that describes how war affected civilians' daily lives. People sometimes said civilians fought on the home front, just as soldiers fought on the front line.

Munitions Weapons.

Nazi party Adolf Hitler's National Socialist (Nazi) Party.

Propaganda Information put out in radio broadcasts, pamphlets, and posters by governments or organizations to change minds or influence what people do.

Radar A method of detecting distant objects, like aircraft and ships, and finding their positions. Stands for "radio detection and ranging."

Rationing A fixed allowance of food, provisions, fuel, and so on, especially in time of scarcity, such as war, set by the government.

Soviet Union The world's first communist state. It existed from 1917–91 and included what is now called Russia. It was also known as the USSR (Union of Soviet Socialist Republics).

Volunteer Someone who chooses to do something rather than being conscripted or called up.

WEB SITES

www.spartacus.schoolnet.co.uk/2WW.htm
A comprehensive site covering every aspect of World War II, including both the military campaigns and the home front.

www.bbc.co.uk/history/worldwars/wwtwo/
The official BBC site on the war, with numerous photographs, maps and spoken word extracts.

www.historyplace.com/worldwar2/timeline/ww2time.htm
A detailed timeline of events from 1918 to the end of World War II, with many photographs.

Index